D1827802

Adrian Bloom's Guide to

TREE FRUIT

text by Peter Blackburne-Maze N.D.H.

Jarrold Colour Publications, Norwich

A pear tree in a mixed border.

Standard trees are too big for most gardens.

Although growing tree fruits (apples, pears, plums, etc.) is becoming more popular these days, they are still not automatically considered for inclusion in the garden in the same way that one would think of shrubs, herbaceous plants, lawns, vegetables and all the other aspects.

This is probably a relic of the days when a single apple tree could take up as much ground as a sizable garage and was regarded more as a place for the children to build a tree-house in rather than as an attractive and productive element of the garden. There was also a certain amount of unwarranted mystique surrounding the subject.

You can still buy trees that will, eventually, become enormous but the demand now is for much smaller ones that can be kept at 6–10 ft high with very little bother. Added to this, many will start cropping the year after planting. Although these developments have been engineered mainly with the commercial fruit grower in mind, we gardeners can benefit from them as well.

Knowing that we can grow tree fruits is one thing, but why should we bother? For a start, a fruit tree offers us a good deal more than most other plants of its size. What other tree has lovely blossom in the spring, developing fruits all through the summer and a really worthwhile, money-saving crop in the autumn? Not many.

Also, tree fruits are simple to grow. Growing fruit is an aspect of gardening that can be made as complicated or as easy as you like but the needs of a tree, if it is to produce a crop, are childishly straightforward. Anyone can grow fruit provided that they are prepared to devote a little time to it. You will find all that you need to know in the following pages.

Sites and Soils

Although commercial fruit growing is mainly confined to the warmer parts of the country below about 400 ft above sea level, perfectly good crops can be grown in less favourable areas but it does mean that more precautions will need to be taken.

Strong winds, for example, are a great hazard to fruit trees, not only causing actual damage to the trees and fruit but also lowering the temperature within the garden considerably. While windbreaks are the obvious answer, solid barriers, such as walls and fences, can, in fact, increase the speed of the wind locally by creating turbulence whereas a hedge will filter it and slow it down.

In these more hostile areas, thought will also have to be given to the types and varieties of fruit that are going to be grown. Not only will spring frosts be a greater danger at blossom time but the summer is likely to be shorter, with the result that the more tender fruits, like peaches and nectarines, are unlikely to ripen in the open.

Sunshine is very desirable, both for raising the temperature and for bringing out the natural colour of the fruits. In cloudy districts, therefore, the less coloured varieties usually do better. Drought is seldom a problem in the United Kingdom but excessive rain can be, and the same consideration ought to be given. Local climatic conditions, such as north-facing slopes which tend to be colder, should also be considered.

One of the most important aspects is the danger that lies in spring frosts. If one of these strikes during blossom time, the chances of a full crop are greatly reduced. This danger is worst in low-lying areas surrounded by high ground or anywhere else where cold air cannot drain away to lower ground. Even a hedge at the bottom of a sloping garden can create such a 'frost pocket'.

In spite of all this, there are very few places where domestic fruit growing is impossible as measures can easily be taken to reduce, or eliminate, the unfavourable aspects. They should never be regarded as barriers, but as points to consider.

Very much the same applies to soils: there are virtually none that cannot be brought up to standard. Ideally, fruit trees should have a well drained yet moisture-retentive soil with a depth of at least 2 ft. It should be slightly acidic (pH 6–6.5) and well supplied with organic matter. In fact, organic matter (garden compost, manure, straw, peat, etc.) is something of an elixir to problem soils in that it opens up clay to improve the drainage, binds together sandy soils so that they retain more moisture and plant foods and improves thin soils overlying chalk beyond all recognition.

Although thin and chalky soils are not ideal for fruit, the younger plum tree in the foreground shows the effect of iron sequestrene.

A well-established bush tree in a commercial orchard. With slightly different pruning, a tree of this size is easily grown in many gardens.

Fruit trees can be bought in virtually any shape or size and, with the smaller gardens of today, the large tree with room enough for the children to play in is fast disappearing. This is not to say that they are unobtainable or should be ignored but it does mean that a great many more of the small trees now available can be grown in the same space without the same problems of shade, maintenance and the wasted ground beneath them. Putting it another way, fruit trees can now be grown where, previously, there was not enough room.

Depending on circumstances and the space available, any of the following tree forms can be grown in gardens:

Standards These make the largest trees of all and are really only suitable for large gardens. The trunk itself is about 6 ft tall and the whole tree can easily reach 30 ft high with a similar spread.

Half-standards Being slightly smaller, these are very effective as specimen trees in a lawn or border as the 4 ft tall trunk leaves plenty of room to work under.

Bush trees These are the smallest trees that do not need special attention in the way of pruning and/or training. They will reach some 12–15 ft high and across with the lowest branches starting 18 in. or so from the ground. They will begin bearing properly when five or six years old and will, ultimately, carry very heavy crops.

4

Dwarf pyramids The smallest 'free-standing' tree form: i.e. not needing to be tied to wires. The height can be restricted to 8–10 ft and the width to 4–5 ft. They crop early in their life and perform best when pruned in summer as well as winter. Really only suitable for apples and pears.

Cordons Also recommended only for apples and pears, these take up less room than any other tree form. Each consists of a single stem on which fruiting spurs are encouraged to develop. They are planted at an angle of 45° against wires or a fence, no branches are allowed to form and both summer and winter pruning are needed if they are to give of their best.

Espalier Another way of training apples and pears against wires or a wall or fence. A central stem is trained vertically and horizontal tiers of opposite branches are trained out at regular intervals. Summer and winter pruning are again required.

Fan-trained Primarily used for stone fruits (plums, peaches, etc.) and figs, in place of the espalier. Instead of a central stem, branches are trained to radiate out from a point near the ground, side shoots being used to fill the spaces created as the main branches get further apart. Both summer and winter pruning are needed.

Other methods of less intensive training, such as **Pillar Trees** and **Spindles**, offer the gardener few advantages over those already described.

Dwarf pyramid.

Cordons.

Espalier.

Fan-trained.

Planning

Fruit trees in a garden must be given ample room in which to grow but must not interfere with the well-being of other plants. They will be there for upwards of twenty years and may often form the 'bones' of the garden around which the other features are built. As mentioned before, they should be in a sheltered position that receives as much sun as possible. Never dump them in an out-of-the-way corner and forget them. For preference, they should be sited towards the north end of a garden where they will be in the sun and yet not cast shade on other plants.

For trees that are going to be trained to a wall or fence, a south or west facing one is best as it provides both sun and warmth. One facing east can be used for the later flowering varieties of apples, pears and plums but the only tree fruit that succeeds well on a north wall is the Morello Cherry, a very sour variety grown solely for cooking.

When trees are trained against wires in the open garden, the rows should, if possible, run in a north–south direction so that both sides catch the sun. In many gardens, they can be used most effectively as a boundary between the ornamental and vegetable sections. In large gardens, it is definitely worthwhile setting aside a special area for fruit. This can combine both free-standing and trained trees as well as all other kinds of fruit. While the trees are building up, the ground between them can be planted with bush fruits (currants and gooseberries) and, during the first few years, even vegetables can be included.

On a smaller scale, greater use should be made of dwarf pyramids and cordons with espalier and fan-trained trees on the walls and fences. Intercropping with vegetables will be possible but harder as there will be much less room between the rows.

Where fruit has to be part of the vegetable garden, the trees should be kept around the sides and full use made of walls and fences for cordons, etc. It may be possible to include larger trees but, as a rule, these are better off in the decorative area. This is also the best plan when no vegetables are grown and trees as large as half-standards can be planted in the lawn or borders to add interest all the year round. In really small gardens, only dwarf pyramids, cordons or trees in pots should be grown.

A young espalier pear.   *Trained plums need more room than this!*

The result of planting too close to a boundary fence. Much of the fruit is unpickable and the tree could be a nuisance to neighbours.

Spacing

Before planting any fruit trees, you must have a good idea of how much room each is going to need. You might already have decided on the form of tree you want (half-standard, bush, cordon, etc.) but a knowledge of how far they should be from each other, and from shrubs and buildings, may mean that you have to change your mind, so be flexible.

Rootstocks determine the vigour and ultimate size of a tree (see p. 10) and this will clearly play a major role in deciding the planting distance. However, other factors must be borne in mind as well, such as the vigour of the actual variety, your own soil conditions and whether the tree is to be planted in a lawn or cultivated ground.

The recommended distances are given in the sections on individual types of fruit but here are some general principles.

1 Never be tempted to plant closer than advised; the trees may look far apart but they will soon grow and fill the space. You can always use the intervening ground for growing other crops in the early years.

2 When planting a tree near a building, allow half the recommended distance between trees and add on about half of that. For example: a tree that should be 12 ft from its neighbour must be 6 ft (half 12) plus 3 ft (half 6), i.e. 9 ft from the nearest building.

3 Where a fence is involved, half the recommended distance between trees is usually enough; in the above case, it would be 6 ft.

4 When planting in grass, leave a circle of cultivated ground about 2 ft in diameter around the base of the tree.

5 Finally: if you are in any doubt about distances, always be on the generous side.

7

Pollination and Fertilisation.

A pretty but crucial time. Wet or cold weather can prevent pollinating insects from doing their job and frost can kill the blossom.

Turning, for a moment, to something a little more technical; the whole object of buying a fruit tree is, of course, to grow your own fruit. Apart from aspects such as correct planting, proper feeding and efficient pest and disease control, a tree will only produce fruit if the flowers have been fertilised. For this to happen, pollen has to be transferred from the male parts of the flower to the female.

Several factors can influence the success of this but the principal one is the weather. For example, a frost can actually destroy the reproductive parts of the flowers, hence the need to guard against spring frosts. However, a more usual problem is that the weather is simply too unpleasant for the normal pollinating insects, such as bees, to be active; hence the need for shelter. Even if pollination does take place, warmth is needed for the pollen to fertilise the flower.

These points can often be catered for by improving local conditions but another thing is that varieties differ in their ability to be fertilised by their own pollen. They can be classified either as fully self-compatible, meaning that they will set a full crop with their own pollen; partially self-compatible, when only a modest crop will be produced; or self-incompatible, when no fruit will form at all. With all but fully self-compatible varieties, therefore, you must have a tree nearby of the same type of fruit but of a different variety so that cross-pollination can take place; details of this are given under the varieties concerned.

Buying Trees

The simple advice here is to buy the best that you can afford. Spread over the life of a tree, which will be at least twenty-five years, a £5–6 outlay is soon brought into perspective; quality is closely allied to price. Fruit trees can be bought in three forms: container grown, bare rooted and root-wrapped.

Container-grown trees, those found in garden centres growing in large polythene pots or something similar, are certainly the most convenient as they can be planted virtually all the year round; but they are also the most expensive. When choosing one, go for a balanced tree that is clearly growing well but which, depending on its age, has also started to fruit. Try to avoid any that are laden with blossom or fruit as they usually lack growth and take a long time to establish. Apart from the usual standards, half-standards and bush trees, you can usually buy ready-trained cordons, espaliers and fan-trained trees.

Bare rooted trees are those that are simply dug up out of the nursery and sold as they are. They can only be bought and planted during the dormant season from November to March. Although four- to five- year-old trees are sometimes obtainable, they are normally much younger and, indeed, for anyone wanting to grow a tree into a specific shape, a maiden (one-year-old) is the best kind to start with.

The third type, root-wrapped trees, come somewhere between the other two in that they are bare rooted trees whose roots have been packed in peat and then sealed in polythene. They are available throughout the dormant season from multiple stores and gardening outlets that do not possess the facilities for bare rooted or container-grown trees. They are frequently kept in warm shops that can encourage them to break into premature growth; for preference, choose those that are completely dormant.

There are many sources of fruit trees, some more trustworthy than others. The safest are garden centres, where you can actually choose your tree, and reliable mail-order

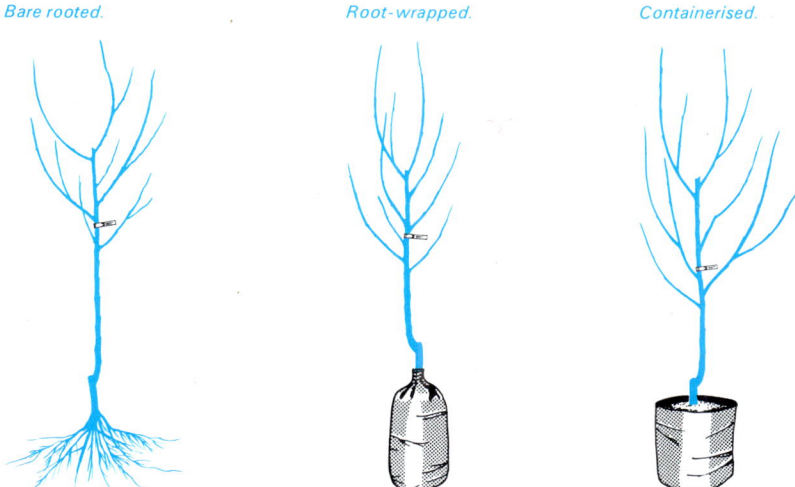

Bare rooted. *Root-wrapped.* *Containerised.*

nurseries whose reputation is all-important to them. There are also smaller specialist nurseries who normally have a wider choice of varieties but fewer kinds of fruit. All these can be relied upon but do beware of small and lavishly worded newspaper adverts offering trees at rock bottom prices; their cheapness may well reflect their quality.

Rootstocks and How Fruit Trees Are Raised

Unlike trees in the wild, cultivated fruit trees do not grow on their own roots. That is to say, the nurseryman propagating a tree will bud or graft some wood of the variety required on to an already growing set of roots; the rootstock. This is done for two main reasons: (*a*) because many tree fruits are difficult to root from cuttings and (*b*) the rootstocks are of known vigour and will determine the rate of growth, the fruitfulness and the eventual size of the tree. For example, standards are grown on vigorous rootstocks whereas dwarf pyramids and cordons are grown on dwarfing ones.

When buying fruit trees, therefore, always make sure that they are growing on a rootstock that will give you a tree of the size and vigour that you want.

Until recently, no truly dwarfing rootstocks were available for stone fruits but these are now being distributed on a limited scale and will shortly be in common use.

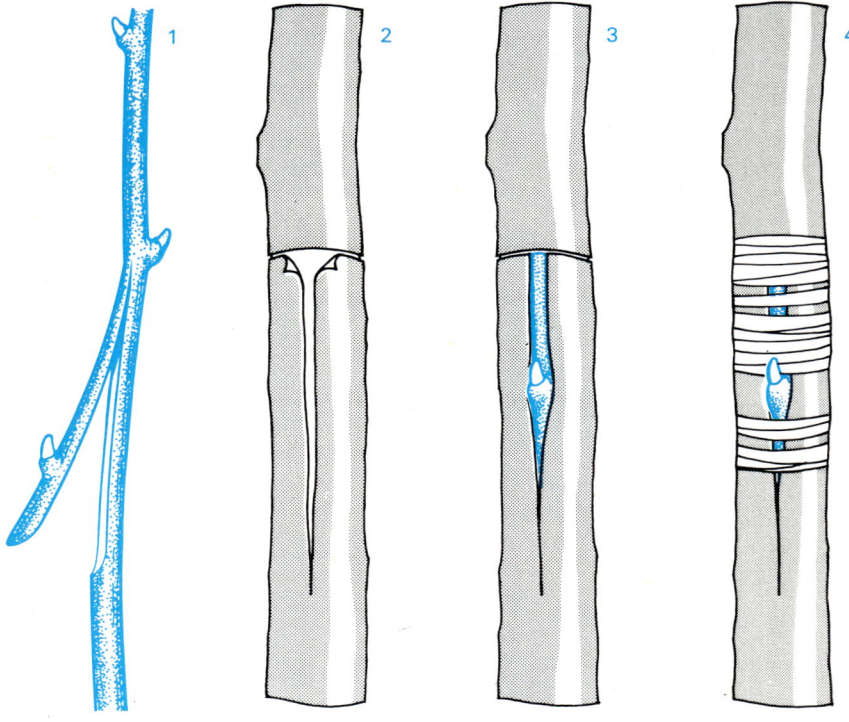

The espalier above is the result of years of careful pruning.

◄ *Budding. (1) A strong bud is taken from the current season's growth. (2) A 'T' cut is made on the rootstock. (3) The bud is pushed well down into the cut. (4) The cut is bound securely with polythene tape.*

Preparations & Planting

As a fruit tree is going to be with you for a great many years, the ground has to be prepared properly; little can be done to improve it later on.

The first essential is to have adequate drainage and good soil to a depth of at least 2 ft. For just one tree, this means preparing a site about 2 ft square, while for a row of cordons a strip of ground 2 ft wide is needed. In both cases, soil should be dug out to a full spade's depth and the underlying subsoil forked as deeply as possible. Where the ground is particularly heavy, it may be necessary to dig out this subsoil and put down a layer of shingle before replacing it but it is normally sufficient to fork in a generous amount of garden compost or manure. The top layer of soil that you dug out should be enriched in the same way but, in addition, a dressing of general fertiliser, such as Growmore, should be mixed in to help the young tree in its first year. A general fertiliser is better than bone meal as it will provide more than just phosphates.

The ground is now ready for planting. The best times for this are November and March but December to February are still all right as long as the weather is reasonable and the soil is in a workable condition (neither frozen nor wet). This dormant period is also best for container-grown trees but these can, in fact, be planted at any time of the year, provided that they can be watered when necessary.

Before actually planting a tree, you must decide if it needs a stake to support it. While all trees will benefit from staking, with some, notably standards, half-standards and those on very dwarfing rootstocks, it is essential if they are to establish quickly and flourish. The reason for staking is not so much to prevent the tree being blown over, though naturally this does come into it, but to stop it blowing about and disturbing the root system.

The correct time to stake is before planting. This avoids the risk of possible root damage by driving it in after planting and it is also easier because you have a hole already dug.

Drive the stake in vertically about 4 in. away from the centre of the hole on the side from which the prevailing wind blows (usually south-west in the United Kingdom); this stops the tree rubbing against the stake.

When planting, spread the roots out evenly, unless the tree is container grown, and make sure that it is at the same depth as it was in the nursery; this is shown by a soil ring a few inches above the roots. On no account bury the bulge at the base of the trunk (the 'union') or roots will form above the rootstock and its effect on the tree's vigour will be lost.

After replacing the first few spadefuls, ensure that the earth falls down between all the roots by joggling the tree about. Also, firm down the soil with your heel as you fill in the hole; never leave it until all the soil is back. Check again that the tree is at the right depth and, using a proper plastic tie, secure it to the stake as high up the main stem as you can, even if it is above the lower branches.

When dealing with single cordons, plant them against their supporting wires at an angle of 45° and with the bulge uppermost; when the tree has reached the top wire, it can then be bent down a further 5° without the risk of it breaking at the union. Finish the job by mulching the ground with a good layer of garden compost.

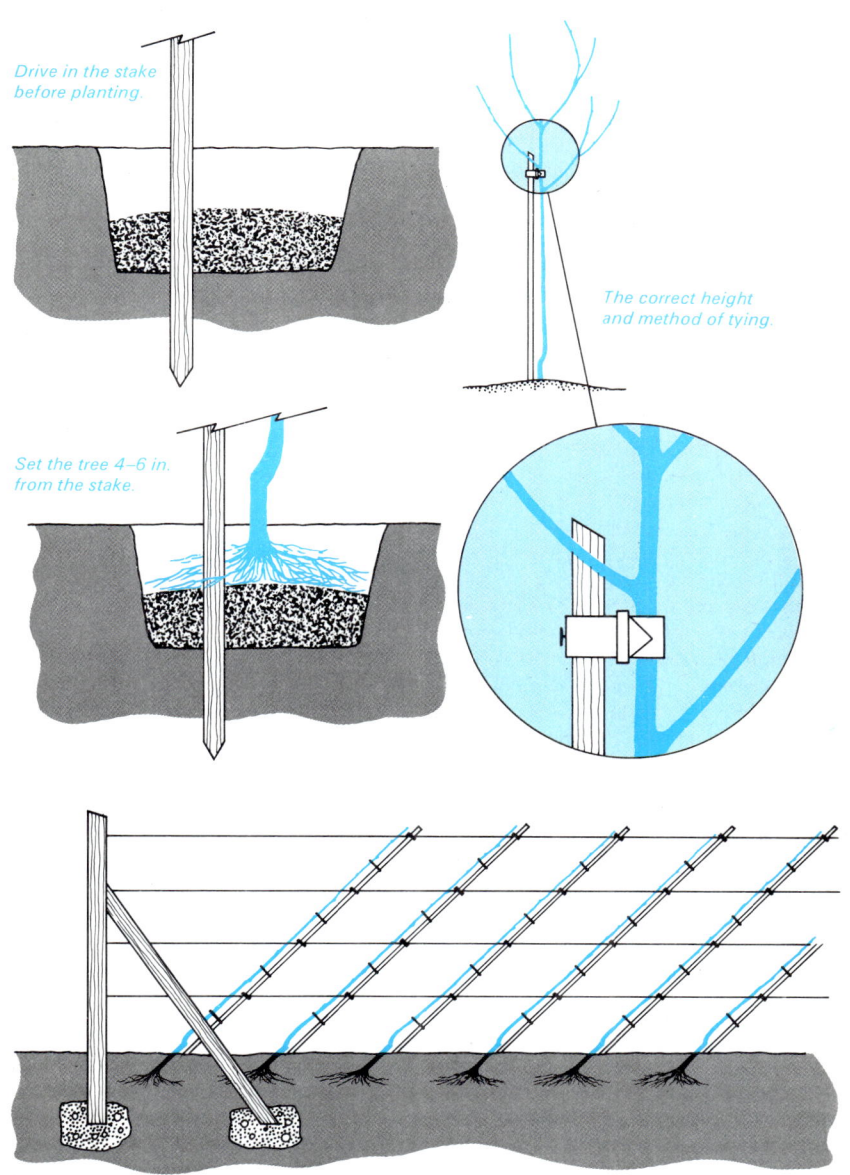

Drive in the stake before planting.

The correct height and method of tying.

Set the tree 4–6 in. from the stake.

Shoots on the cordon on the left are trained towards the post.

13

Another fine example of the pruner's art. A fan-trained tree that is both attractive and fruitful. This system is recommended for all stone fruits (plums, cherries, peaches, etc.) and figs.

To support cordons, espaliers and fan-trained trees, a system of horizontal wires will be needed, preferably stranded as opposed to single wire. For cordons, these should be 3, 5 and 7 ft above the ground; espaliers will need them a foot apart, starting from about 18 in. high, while for fan-trained trees they should be every 6–9 in. When grown in the open garden and not against a wall, 10-ft-long supporting posts are driven 3 ft into the ground or set in concrete and spaced every 10 ft along the row. The end posts should be strutted for extra strength.

Maintenance

Manures and Fertilisers

The need to feed fruit trees is just as great as it is to feed any other crop and the soil must also be in good condition or the roots will be unable to operate effectively. Mulching the surface of the ground around the trees every spring with garden compost or farmyard manure is the simplest way of maintaining the soil in good condition but it can also be done by lightly digging in the same materials, care being taken not to damage the roots.

The really important element to all fruit crops is potash, for it is this that encourages fruitfulness. The fertilisers normally rich in potash are tomato and rose foods. As a rule, rose foods are preferable, particularly when the trees are surrounded by grass, as they contain more nitrogen, another vital element.

The best time to apply a fertiliser depends on the size and age of the tree. Large, well established trees will have a very deep root system so fertiliser should go on in January or early February to allow it to be washed down to the roots before growth starts. With recently planted trees, however, late March is more appropriate. Trees of other ages will clearly come between these two dates.

Pest and Disease Control

No matter how well a tree is looked after, it will inevitably attract a variety of pests and diseases throughout each growing season. While the table over the page will show you how to recognise and control the main ones, a certain number of general points are important if good results are to be had.

1 Look at the trees frequently so that trouble can be spotted before it gets out of hand.
2 Identify the problem positively and correctly.
3 Choose the right chemical, or other means, to control the outbreak.
4 Always spray thoroughly using the recommended dilution rate.
5 Avoid spraying during windy weather and bright sunlight.
6 Never use insecticides during blossom since most will kill bees.
7 Always read and understand the instructions on the pack before spraying.

◀ *Left to right: A pint sprayer for small trees and gardens. An aerosol for isolated outbreaks. A one-gallon sprayer for larger gardens.*

Captions for illustrations overleaf in an anticlockwise direction and starting at top left, are as follows:

Apple scab; Codling Moth caterpillar; Apple Mildew; Apple Sawfly maggots; Apple Sawfly scars; the result of good pest and disease control; storage rot; Brown Rot of plums; Capsid scars. ▶

15

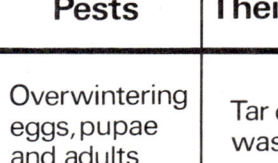

see page 15 for picture captions

Period (Month)	Pests	Their
Dormant (Nov – Feb)	Overwintering eggs, pupae and adults	Tar oi| wash|
Pre-blossom (Mar – May)	Greenfly, Blackfly and Apple sucker	A sys| insect|
	Caterpillars and Capsids	Linda|
	Apple sawfly	Linda| petal	
Fruitlet (June – Aug)	Codling moth	Perme| late J|
	Red spider mite	Dime|
Harvest (Sept – Oct)	Wasp nests	Carba| pirimi| meth|

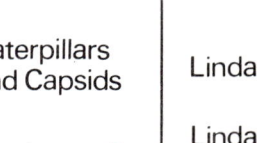

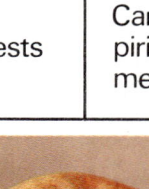

Diseases	Their control
Canker etc.	Cut out and burn dead and diseased shoots and branches
Peach leaf curl	A copper fungicide at bud−burst
Apple mildew	Benomyl, bupirimate or dinocap
Apple and Pear Scab	Benomyl, thiophanate− methyl or captan
Storage rots	Benomyl or thiophanate before picking

Pruning

We can start thinking of pruning the moment a tree is planted as there will very probably be some shoots that are damaged. These have to be cut back to below the point of injury. Proper pruning can then start.

With any fruit tree, pruning during the first few winters must be aimed solely at shaping it and building it up; pruning for fruit will come later.

BUILDING THE TREE (*See pruning diagrams on pages 20 and 21*)
Standard, half-standard and bush are the most popular forms of untrained fruit trees and all are dealt with very similarly be they apples, pears, plums, cherries or peaches.

If the tree you are buying is a one-year-old (a maiden), it is cut back to 2 ft high to form a bush tree (1), 4 ft for a half-standard and, if necessary, allowed to grow on to 6 ft for a standard. In some cases, the stem will already have side-shoots (feathers) growing from it and, if these are just below where you make the cut, three or four of them can be used to start forming branches by shortening them to 4–5 in. long. All feathers not appropriately placed are cut off.

The following winter, only those shoots that are to form the main branches are retained (2). Choose four or five of the best placed and cut them back by one third to an outward pointing bud. All others are cut out. In a year's time, the resulting eight to ten shoots are again cut back by about one third and you have the main framework of the tree with a nice open centre.

Dwarf pyramids, on the other hand, are based on a main central stem. Apples, pears and plums can all be grown in this way but apples that carry their fruit on the tips of the shoots, such as Worcester and Laxton's Superb, are not really suitable.

Starting with an unfeathered maiden, simply cut the stem to 20 in. high. If feathered, though, cut it back to about 9 in. above the top feather (3) and shorten them all to 5–6 in.; any that are less than 9 in. from the ground are cut right off. Always prune the feathers to a downward pointing bud. The following winter, the new upper shoots on previously unfeathered trees are cut back to 8 in. and this is graded down to 10 in. for the lower ones (4). On all trees, extension growth on the main stem is cut back to about 1 ft to a bud pointing in the opposite direction to that of the previous winter; this will maintain a straight stem.

Thereafter, any new side-shoots growing directly from the main stem are cut back to 5 in., or removed if likely to cause overcrowding. On the branches, extension growth is shortened to 5 in. and any side-shoots to 2–3 in. Once the tree is three–four years old, summer as well as winter pruning will be needed.

For cordons, the main stem can be left unpruned if there are plenty of feathers and these are shortened to 3 in. long (5). Any that are less than 12 in. from the ground are removed. Where there are no feathers, the main stem is shortened by about one quarter to encourage side-shoots. From then on, all pruning is done in the summer (6).

PRUNING ESTABLISHED TREES

Clearly, space is too limited here to go into all the different methods of pruning fully but, as far as most standard, half-standard and bush trees are concerned, the three main systems are Regulated, Renewal and Spur.

Regulated pruning is the simplest and is equally good for apples, pears, plums and cherries. In essence, it involves making a small number of large cuts with a saw rather than snipping away with secateurs. Fortunately, it is fairly straightforward to

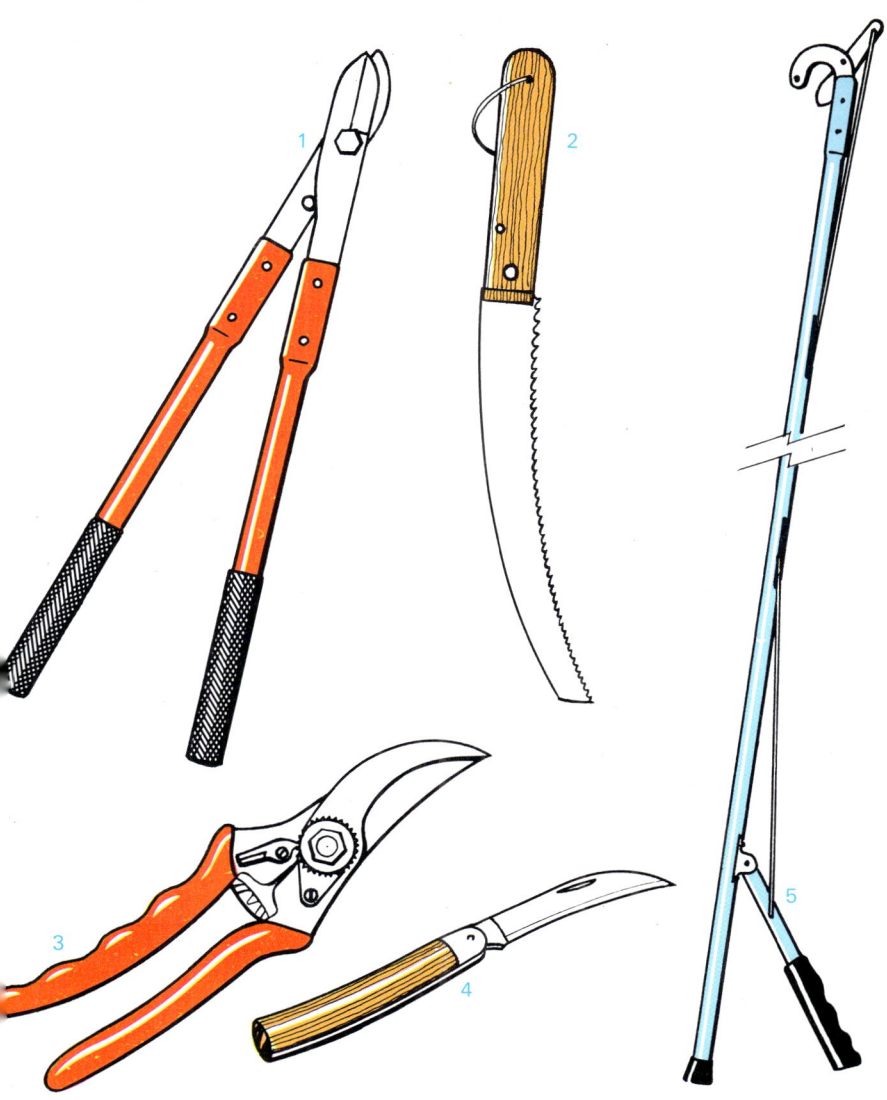

Pruning tools. Loppers (1) are useful for cutting off branches too awkward for a proper pruning saw (2) but too large for secateurs (3). They should always be used with the cutting blade towards the tree to avoid the bark being crushed. A strong knife (4) must be used to pare all large saw cuts. Both this and the secateurs must be kept really sharp. For tall trees, a 'long-arm' pruner (5) is indispensable.

determine which branches should go. The important ones are those that are dead, broken or badly diseased, any that are causing obvious overcrowding and those that are crossing the tree from one side to the other. Add to these any that are spoiling the shape of the tree or are growing too high and it could well be that nothing else needs removing. Always remember, though, to protect saw cuts with a fungicidal paint and to leave plum and cherry pruning until as late in the dormant season as possible; this greatly reduces the risk of fungal infection.

Renewal pruning is certainly the best method for standard, half-standard and bush trees of apples and pears and consists of forming a more or less permanent framework of branches on which are borne fruiting shoots of varying ages. Pruning is aimed at building up new fruiting shoots as the older ones become less productive.

Because a shoot will crop sooner and better if it is only lightly pruned, little is needed beyond removing the tips of the shoots. This leads to much more flexible branches which, when they have bent down far enough to be a nuisance, are cut back to a strong shoot on the upper surface.

Spur pruning is the very opposite in that a lasting and rigid branch system is built up on which fruiting spurs are encouraged to form. All leading shoots (the principal and dominant one on the end of each branch) are cut back every winter by about one third. New side-shoots growing directly from a branch are cut back to four buds and those growing from stumps that have already been treated thus are cut back to one bud. In this way, a spur system is built up.

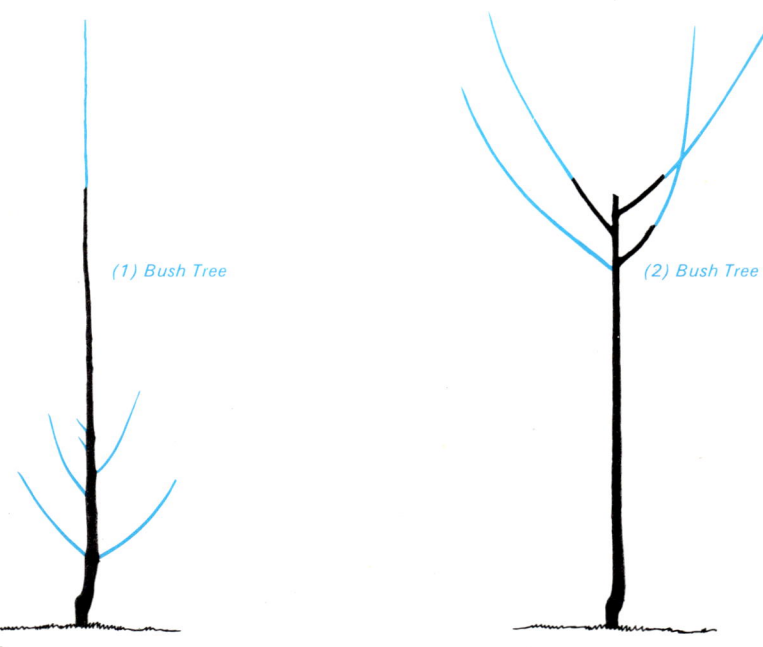

(1) Bush Tree

(2) Bush Tree

20

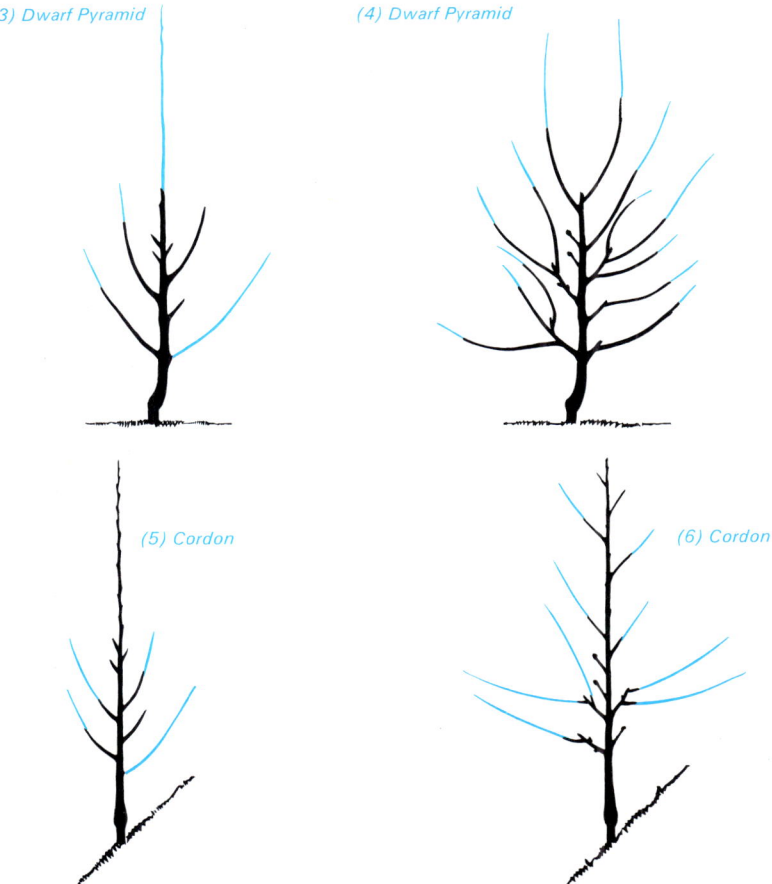

(3) Dwarf Pyramid

(4) Dwarf Pyramid

(5) Cordon

(6) Cordon

A method of pruning that is particularly worthwhile with cordon, espalier and dwarf pyramid apples and pears is carried out in the summer with a view to reducing growth and encouraging fruitfulness. Pruning takes place between mid-July and mid-August, depending on your location, when the new shoots are 12–18 in. long and are starting to harden up.

All shoots growing from the main stem of cordons or the branches of espaliers and pyramids are cut back to 3 in. Those growing from existing side-shoots or spurs go back to 1 in. Any shoot that is immature at that time is left for a month before being pruned.

Those are the main methods of pruning fruit trees and you will find them referred to again in the Fruit section.

Picking & Storage

Most fruits should be allowed to ripen on the tree, be picked by lifting and twisting (when they should part easily), and then be eaten within a few days of picking. Many apples and pears, though, can be stored for up to six months, depending on the variety.

Variety	Ready for picking	Ready to eat
Apples (eating)		
Cox	Late Sept–early Oct	October–December
Egremont Russet	Early October	November–December
Ellison's Orange	September	October–November
Charles Ross	Early October	November–December
Ashmead's Kernel	Late October	April–May
Apples (cooking)		
Bramley	Late Sept–early Oct	October–February
Howgate Wonder	Late September	October–January
Lane's Prince Albert	Late Sept–early Oct	November–March
Pears		
Conference	September	October–November
Comice	October	November
Glou Morceau	October	December–January
Pitmaston Duchess	September	October–November

When picking, care must be taken to avoid damaging the fruit, especially if intended for storage, as wounds and bruises soon become infected. Apples and pears can be stored in several ways, the simplest, for small lots, certainly being in the bottom of the fridge, providing the temperature stays **above freezing**. For larger quantities, apples (not pears) can be stored in polythene bags (these should not be sealed, but simply fold the open end under) or wrapped in newspaper and stored in boxes. Pears like fresh air around them and are best laid out on shelves or racks. In all cases, the fruit must be kept as cool as possible from the moment it is picked. A brick garage or shed is fine for this; a cellar is the best place of all. Keep an eye on the fruit during storage and remove any that are showing signs of deterioration.

Small quantities of fruit can be stored in polythene bags (left) but larger amounts should be wrapped in newspaper (right)

Restoring Neglected Trees

Trim and paint all saw cuts.

A neglected tree before (top) and after (bottom) pruning.

A forgotten tree is easily recognised; its branches form a sort of aerial undergrowth, a fair percentage of them are dead, growth is virtually at a standstill and any crops are light with individual fruits small and often diseased.

The first essential is to get the tree growing again and this is largely done by winter pruning. Where there are clearly far too many branches, this is better carried out over two winters rather than just one. Pruning should be done along the lines of the regulated system (page 18).

There will certainly be a build-up of moss, lichen and pests on the tree so pruning should be followed by a tar oil winter wash. Routine spraying during the growing season with an insecticide and fungicide will also be needed. A general fertiliser, such as Growmore, should be given annually in the spring.

The result of all this should be a profusion of new shoots but only those that you want to develop into branches are retained. These are shortened by about a third to encourage side-shoots and are eventually built up as replacements for the older and worn out ones.   There are instances, of course, when a tree is just 'past it'; the main criterion being the number of dead branches. If, after removing these, the picture is pretty grim, you seriously ought to consider replacing the tree with a new one as this is usually a far better proposition; flogging a dead horse is a waste of time. If a tree of this sort is a particular favourite and the variety, if known, is unobtainable, contact a local nursery; they are often willing to grow you a new tree using material from the old one.

Inducing Fruitfulness

Besides neglect, there can be many reasons for a tree failing to fruit. Excessive vigour is a very common cause, usually brought on by one or more of the following:

1 Planting too deep so that the union is buried (page 12). Solution – Dig away the soil from the base of the tree to expose the union and sever any roots growing out from above it.

2 Too vigorous a rootstock for the size of tree required. Solution – Apply only fertilisers that are rich in potash, such as tomato or rose foods.

3 A combination of vigorous rootstock and fertile soil. Solution – As 2.

4 Pruning too hard. Solution – Change to a lighter method.

Give these remedies at least a year to work. If they appear to be quite ineffective after that time, bark-ringing should have the desired effect or, as a last resort, root pruning.

Trees sometimes fail to blossom; this could be the result of:

1 Excessive vigour. See above.

2 Too shaded a position. Solution – Remove the cause of the shading or, if impossible, replant elsewhere.

3 Underfeeding. Solution – Apply the recommended amount of a suitable fertiliser every spring.

4 Removal of the fruit buds by bullfinches, etc. during the winter. Solution – if the trees are young, net them from November until the buds are opening in the spring; if old, treat them periodically with a proprietary chemical deterrent.

The reward of good managment. A crop of Doyenne du Comice pears; not the easiest to grow.

If the tree blossoms but fails to set fruit, the most likely cause is that a sharp spring frost killed the flowers; however, underfeeding is also possible.

When fruit is formed but fails to develop and drops after a few weeks, the tree is probably underfed and/or the soil is too dry. With apples, it can even be brought on by a serious attack of Apple sawfly (see centre pages).

Two last resorts for reducing vigour. Left, root pruning and, right, bark ringing. These methods should be read up before attempting them as they could result in doing more harm than good.

Types & Varieties

Cox

Spartan

APPLES

These are undoubtedly the most widely planted tree fruit, mainly because our soil and climate enables us to grow them better than anyone else. It also allows us to breed and grow the finest varieties in the world. Do you know that around 6,000 distinct varieties have been or still are grown here?

Spacing

This should be considered at the planning stage because, without adequate room to grow, no tree will flourish.

Standards and half-standards	Not less than 18 ft (5·5 m apart)
Bush trees. Semi-vigorous	12–18 ft (3·5–5·5 m apart)
Semi-dwarfing	10–15 ft (3–4·5 m apart)
Dwarfing rootstock	8–10 ft (2·5–3 m apart)
Dwarf pyramids	3–4 ft (1–1·25 m apart)
Cordons	2·5–3·5 ft (0·75–1 m apart)
Espaliers. Dwarfing rootstock	10–12 ft (3–3·5 m apart)
Semi-dwarfing	12–15 ft (3·5–4·5 m apart)
Vigorous	15–18 ft (4·5–5·5 m apart)

Varieties

While many others will be found in nurseries and garden centres, most of them perfectly good, all the following are notable either for their heavy crops, regular cropping or high quality fruit. (D)=Dessert; (C)=Cooking.

Cox's Orange Pippin (D) Probably the finest apple available but not a very reliable cropper. Suitable for all tree forms and, as a bush tree or larger, responds well to renewal pruning. Susceptible to Mildew.

Greensleeves (D) A new variety with a slightly later season than Cox. Of Golden Delicious appearance but with a better flavour. It makes a compact tree that crops early in its life. A good and reliable cropper. Well pollinated by Cox and Egremont Russet.

Spartan (D) A Canadian apple that crops regularly and heavily, the fruit being a very dark red and of good flavour. It stores until Christmas. The trees are rather susceptible to Canker. Well pollinated by Cox and Discovery and a good pollinator for Cox, Discovery and Bramley.

Discovery (D) An excellent early apple that is largely replacing Worcester. Rather slow to crop but with good fruit size in a warm season. Keeps for several weeks after picking. A moderately vigorous tree that fruits well on the spurs. Well pollinated by Cox, Spartan and Greensleeves.

Orleans Reinette (D) A very old variety of first rate quality that is fit to eat in December and January but not a reliable or heavy cropper. A strong grower suitable for bush trees or espaliers. A variety for the specialist rather than the average gardener.

Charles Ross and Red Charles Ross (D) Another old variety, though the red 'sport' is newer. The fruit is large, attractive and of good flavour. It makes a fairly upright tree and is suitable for dwarf forms when grown on a dwarfing rootstock. Cox pollinates it well.

Ashmead's Kernel (D) A very old variety, keeping well into March. Excellent flavour but a poor cropper. It makes a fairly compact tree.

Kidd's Orange Red (D) A New Zealand apple with Cox as one parent. Cox-like flavour and a regular and heavy cropper with an attractive half-russeted skin. In season from November to February. Slightly more vigorous than Cox.

Egremont Russet (D) Crops well when young but rather erratic when older. In season from mid-October till early December. A nice golden russet covers most or all of the fruit which is of medium size and good flavour. A strong and upright tree that is well pollinated by Cox and Greensleeves.

Egremont Russet   *Grenadier*

Ellison's Orange (D) An October apple that is liable to crop every other year if not properly managed. Juicy with a slightly aniseed flavour. Fairly resistant to spring frosts. The tree is of moderate vigour and quite upright. Cox is one of its parents.

Fortune (D) Another offspring of Cox but an earlier variety that ripens in late September. A variable cropper that prefers the sunnier south and east. Juicy and of very good flavour. Moderately vigorous, producing a fairly upright tree.

Rosemary Russet (D) An excellent and old late apple that keeps until February. A very rich flavour and of moderate growth and fertility.

Early Victoria/Emneth Early (C) The earliest cooking apple and not grown nearly widely enough; in many years it can be picked at the end of July. A long apple of typical codlin appearance. A reliable and quite heavy cropper that makes an upright tree which responds well to Spur pruning.

Grenadier (C) Another early variety (August–September) that is a slow grower but regular cropper. Very resistant to Scab. A good pollinator for Bramley and well pollinated by Spartan.

Lane's Prince Albert (C) One of the most reliable croppers and in season from December to February. A small and spreading tree that is well suited to gardens. Susceptible to Mildew but fairly resistant to Scab. Self-fertile.

Howgate Wonder (C) A heavy and regular cropper that keeps until late February. Not a first-rate cooker but the fruits are very large. The tree is vigorous, which makes it rather unsuitable for small gardens.

Bramley Seedling (C) Although probably the best cooker of all, this is only a variety to grow where there is plenty of room as it can make a very large tree. The normal season is from November to February but it often keeps much longer. The pollen is sterile so it is useless as a pollinator.

Family Trees For some years now, fruit trees have been available that have been grafted with three varieties instead of one, as is customary. These are produced in various mixtures and are of enormous benefit to the owners of small gardens who want a number of varieties but lack the room for a tree of each. For example, just two family trees can give you a supply of apples from August until well into the New Year.

Howgate Wonder   *Bramley*

Conference Pear

PEARS

Pear trees are normally grown on Quince rootstock.

Spacing

Bush trees and espaliers	12–15 ft (3·5–4·5 m apart)
Dwarf pyramids	3–4 ft (1–1·25 m apart)
Cordons	2–3 ft (0·6–1 m apart)

Varieties

Conference (D) Certainly the most popular and appropriate pear for gardens where only one variety is wanted. It will partially pollinate itself but will even produce fruits without being pollinated. It is a regular and heavy cropper. It is moderately vigorous and the fruit is at its best in November and early December.

Onward (D) A new variety that has Comice as one parent. It is in season in the second half of September and early October between Williams and Conference. The fruit is juicy and of excellent flavour. The tree is vigorous and forms fruiting spurs readily. It blossoms late, thus often avoiding spring frosts.

William's Bon Chrétien (D) A very old variety that spurs freely and is of only moderate vigour. It crops regularly but not heavily and is in season during the first half of September; one of the earliest. Unfortunately, the fruit only stays in good condition for a very short time.

Glou Morceau (D) One of the finest late pears, ripening in December and January. The tree is moderately vigorous and rather spreading. A very reasonable cropper that is at its best when grown against a south- or west-facing wall or fence.

Pitmaston Duchess (D) A large pear that ripens in October and November. The skin is slightly coarse but the flesh is sweet and juicy. The large and spreading tree crops well and regularly.

Doyenne du Comice (D) Probably the finest pear of all but not too regular a cropper. It has a delicious flavour and ripens in November. The tree is only moderately vigorous but the uncertain cropping allows it to grow quite tall. (See page 25.)

Catillac (C) A very late cooking pear that will keep till April. It crops well but makes a large and strong tree. One of the best culinary varieties, it cooks to a deep red.

Family trees of pears are also quite widely available.

PLUMS AND GAGES

Technically, plums are for cooking and gages for dessert but many plums make good 'eaters' and there are a lot of dual-purpose varieties. Unfortunately, blossoming is early in the year so damage from spring frosts is common.

Although St Julien A is the most commonly used rootstock, a very much more dwarfing one, Pixy, is becoming available, which will allow plums to be far more widely grown where space is limited.

Spacing

Bush trees on	St Julien A	15–20 ft (4·5–6 m apart)
	Pixy	8–10 ft (2·5–3 m apart
Half-standards		18–25 ft (5·5–7·5 m apart)
Dwarf pyramids	St Julien A	10–12 ft (3–3·5 m apart)
	Pixy	6–7 ft (approx. 2 m apart)
Fan-trained		15–18 ft (4·5–5·5 m apart)

Varieties

Czar An early, dark blue cooking plum (early August) of reasonable dessert quality. The tree is compact and not vigorous. A reliable cropper and pollinates itself.

Victoria Ripening in late August, this is the best variety for gardens. A heavy cropper that does not need cross-pollination. Although primarily a cooker, it can be treated as a dessert if left to ripen fully. A moderately sized, fairly vigorous and rather drooping tree.

Jefferson A delicious dessert variety that is ready for use early in September. A moderately vigorous tree that needs cross-pollination for good crops. The fruit is yellow flushed with red.

Early Transparent Gage A mid-August variety of very high dessert quality. The tree is small and cross-pollination is not necessary. A good variety.

Green Gage Possibly the finest dessert variety but, most unfortunately cropping is light and unreliable. In a large garden, this is a 'must'. It ripens in late August to early September and tree growth is moderate.

Cambridge Gage Similar in most respects to the Green Gage but larger all round and more reliable cropping, though of inferior flavour.

Victoria Plum

Jefferson Gage

Peregrine peach. All peaches and nectarines succeed better against a wall or fence and often need protecting from birds and wasps. Look at the right-hand fruit!

CHERRIES

Until recently, cherries could not be recommended for gardens as the trees grew far too large and cross-pollination was essential. However, a semi-dwarfing rootstock, Colt, is slowly becoming more widespread and there is a new variety, **Stella,** that is self-fertile. At the moment, this is the most suitable combination for gardens unless there is sufficient room for the larger trees and more than one variety.

The **Morello** cherry is also perfectly satisfactory but no attempt should be made to eat it raw! It is essentially a cooker but it has the virtue of fruiting well when trained to a north-facing wall.

PEACHES

While these are sometimes grown in the open as bush trees, they are far more reliable when fan-trained against a south- or west-facing wall or fence. Hand pollination and protection from spring frosts are essential if good crops are to be had. Peaches are almost entirely grown on St Julien A rootstock.

Peregrine (early August) is the most suitable variety, with **Rochester** (Mid-August) as a good alternative.

Beware of the fungus disease Peach Leaf Curl.

FIGS

Although not to everyone's liking, figs certainly add variety to a fruit collection and, while they are often grown in the open, they definitely benefit from the protection of a wall. They also have very large and attractive leaves. Figs are grown on their own roots.

Before investing in a tree, I suggest you try eating a fresh fig that is at the peak of ripeness and just about to split. The most reliable and prolific variety is **Brown Turkey;** it ripens from mid-August onwards.